Paw Prints in My Heart

A devotional book

with everyday lessons of life inspired by my
dear pet, companion and friend, Leo

Barbara Zimmerman

Fresh Cup Publishing
Edmond, Oklahoma

Dedication and Special Thanks

This book is dedicated to Mom and Dad, who instilled in me a loving respect for animals. Their passion for reading and writing has become mine as well.

Above all, I give thanks to Jesus Christ for inspiring these devotionals through the Holy Spirit. He is my constant Friend and Teacher. May He receive all the glory!

Thank you, fellow dog lovers, for encouraging me.

A special thanks to Katherine Spurgeon, Melissa French, and Debbie Klassen for taking the time to proofread the original manuscript.

Thank you, Darla Hunter, for editing, and Victor Driver, for updating the book cover. You both did an outstanding job!

Thank you, the reader, for reading my book. My prayer is that you will be drawn closer to Jesus Christ, the Lord, as you read each page. God bless you.

Contents

Good Gift 1

Content 2

Eager to Please 3

Mr. Brown Eyes 4

Bath Time 5

Dirty Feet 6

Asleep in the Shade 7

Going for a Walk 8

Night Walks 9

Expectancy 10

Fresh Oil 11

Just Sitting 12

Similarities 13

The Door 14

A Licking 15

Resting 16

Prepared Place 17

Skunk Expert 18

Collar Time 19

A Touch 20

Clean Teeth 21

Shaven 22

Wellness Plan 23

Looking in the Mirror 24

Playtime 25

Happy Trails 26

Moving On 27

The Ride..28

Sunning..29

Chewer 30

Mark of the Beast 31

Pretty Doggie..32

Receiver 33

Following 34

Storms...35

Senior 36

Perky Ears..37

Just a Glance..38

The Dewed..39

Toys 40

Sleepless..41

The Brushing 42

Fearless..43

Walking in the Snow 44

Eating Habits 45

Country Break 46

On Guard...47

Lost and Found...48

To the Lake or Bust 49

Attacked! 50

Pain in the Paw...51

Comforter..52

How many are your works, O Lord!
In wisdom you made them all;
The earth is full of your creatures…
Living things both large and small.

— Psalm 104:24,25 (NIV)

Good Gift

Over the years, I have received many precious gifts. I won't take time to enumerate the valuable items and priceless relationships I have received. Instead, I desire to call attention to what a precious gift Leo has been to me. He has brought such joy and playfulness back into my life. His companionship has been a comfort. The fact was that I desired Leo to be mine for about three years before he became mine. The Lord knew my heart longing and gave me a registered, beautifully marked, gentle Sheltie. Leo was one of my gifts from the Lord.

Good and perfect gifts (James 1:17) come to us from a generous Heavenly Father. Jesus was the ultimate Gift. When He came, we began to understand the giving nature of God. Through Jesus, God gave us salvation, healing, deliverance, joy, peace, love, and so much more. In the one Gift of Jesus, we have been given eternal life. What a good Gift! What a good gift Giver!

Content

Leo was content just to be with me. Although his constant plea was to be touched, if I was busy he simply chose to be nearby. What a peaceful image when he'd lie down in that spot near or under my chair. "All is well; life is swell" could be the caption for this picture of Leo, my pet Sheltie. I found delight in providing such a peaceful environment for him.

I can relate to the desire of the Shepherd in Psalm twenty-three when "He makes me to lie down in green pastures." A peaceful picture of contentment comes to mind. The sheep are well fed and watered and then lie down in green pastures where plenty abounds. Because the Lord is indeed my Shepherd, I should have caught on that all is well, but I am a slow learner. After all these years, I should know I have everything when I am near the Shepherd. You've got one over on me, Leo!

Eager to Please

I knew I couldn't have Leo's heart transplanted into me but, in a sense, I would like that. He was so eager to please and obey me! Sometimes I rewarded Leo with a treat to eat and other times his reward was a word of praise and vigorous petting. He didn't seem to care what his reward was because he had a deep, driving desire just to please me.

I find myself lacking in that area when it comes to responding to the Lord's requests and commands. The Lord has promised so many rewards for seeking Him and obeying Him. His rewards are rich, abundant, and eternal in nature, better than doggie treats. Even so, I find myself choosing to please myself or another person rather than my Creator and Savior. Something's wrong with this picture. Once again, I am challenged. My friend Leo stirred up a desire to please my Friend Jesus. It's humbling to be taught by a dog.

Mr. Brown Eyes

It was difficult for Leo when I closed the bathroom door to take my evening shower. As soon as I opened the door, I found him looking up at me with those soft brown eyes. It seemed to be almost a look of relief, as if I went somewhere and finally returned. Come to think of it, whenever I was home, I was under his watchful eye. First, he had to be where I was. Then, when he saw me, he relaxed and lay down to sleep.

How much more effectively does our Father keep His eyes on us? He can see beyond any closed door and even into our hearts. It is so comforting to know such continuous care from our God Who never sleeps or slumbers (Psalm 121: 4). Thanks for reminding me, Mr. Brown Eyes.

Bath Time

Leo's previous owner said he hated water and refused to be given a bath. Based on that information, I decided to have the groomer bathe him first. The groomer told me Leo was afraid, but he had no problems in bathing him. The next time, I braved the experience myself. Once in the bathtub, Leo was compliant and docile as I soaped, lathered, and rinsed him. In fact, he stood there patiently during the entire process, eager, of course, for the final rinse and great escape from the tub. Each time since then has been easier and more enjoyable.

When it comes time for me to be under the mighty hand of God for cleansing, instruction, and direction, am I easy or a challenge to handle? Leo in the bathtub is an example to keep in mind, and yet I am ready for the "great escape." Aren't you?

Dirty Feet

Sometimes I think dogs and dirty feet were meant to go together. The problem was that dirty feet and a clean house were not compatible. Leo so enjoyed running along the fence as he socialized with the neighbor dogs, he had erased all the grass and replaced it with a bare dirt path. In the mornings, his running sprees caused his feet to look like unsettled brownie mix: a little dew mixed with just enough dirt. Leo couldn't come in the house dirty, so I cleaned his feet almost daily, just so I could have him near me when I was home.

The Father has a similar dilemma. He desires to have us close and yet our sin and His holiness don't mix. His remedy is the Blood of Jesus that has the power to cleanse us from all unrighteousness, so we can draw near to the Father. The Father enjoys our company like I enjoy Leo's (probably even more). His Son paid the cleansing price, so that our "dirty feet" could become "happy feet" in His Presence.

Asleep in the Shade

There were several mandatory feats to conquer, being a small dog who owned a large backyard. First, he had to meet his neighbors and mark his territory in their face, or at least within the range of their smell. Then, barking and chasing were necessary to maintain rulership. Leo stirred up much dust along our fence lines establishing his boundaries. After he finished his important job, Leo came over to the paved patio area and slept under my chair.

What a picture of rest and peace to see Leo asleep under my chair. The heat of his battle was over. He rested secure. In the same way, we need to rest in the shadow of our almighty conquering Lord and Savior. When all is said and done, He is the Greater One. We are in His shadow: safe, at rest, and content. The boundaries are established; the victories are won. Come join me on the patio.

Going for a Walk

Leo's previous owners told us he wouldn't go for a walk because he didn't like being on a leash. That was disheartening to someone who wanted a walking companion. Fortunately, our neighbor was experienced in training dogs and was willing to help with this dilemma. Within a week, Leo was leash trained, but it was a grueling process. At first, he was literally dragged on his back in resistance. It didn't take long, though, for him to get on his feet in compliance. From that point on, he has been willing to learn how and really enjoys walking on a leash. Now, I can't even say the word "walk" without him excitedly barking and prancing about with anticipation.

When the Lord asks me to walk with Him, what is my response? Do I lie down in resistance and cower in fear? Walking in the unknown and unseen has admittedly been a hindrance to my enthusiasm. Why? The Lord of All has invited me to walk and fellowship with Him. What's with the fear? Did someone say, "Walk?" Let's go!

Night Walks

When I first took Leo for walks, he was absorbed with watching me as he happily pranced along. I guess he was checking to see if everything was okay. After a month or so, however, he became more confident in his expertise as a walker and would get easily distracted by people, noises, and other dogs. During our night walks, though, I noticed his attention zeroed back on me. He couldn't see all the distractions and was more dependent on my guidance.

Although it's frustrating, the Lord has chosen that we walk by faith. He alone knows where we're going and how we're getting there. We are totally dependent on Him, His guidance, and His ability to see what we cannot. Just like Leo, these walks make us remain close to our Companion. Somehow, I am convinced that the Lord likes it that way. In fact, I know He does!

Expectancy

Leo was the embodiment of enthusiastic expectancy. Whenever I was awake and around, he seemed to expect something: a pat, a treat, a walk, a word, or simply my companionship. Oddly enough, his expectations caused me to respond. When he looked at me, nuzzled my hand, or just wagged his tail, I responded. I enjoyed his attention as much as he enjoyed mine.

Expectant faith works much the same way. The Lord responds to me when I look to Him with anticipation. As I just delight in and want to be with Him, He in turn delights in and draws near to me. He responds to my faith as I hopefully wait for a word, a reward, or a touch. As I look to Him expecting to receive, He responds. Strange how a "tail-wagger" could encourage my faith, but he did.

Fresh Oil

When I was a child, I remember washing our dog in an old washtub in the back yard. The soap was slippery and hard to hang onto when it was wet. Supposedly, it had the double action of cleaning the dog and killing the fleas. As far as I recall, it worked. After shopping for Leo, however, I learned that liquid soap had replaced bar soap and special oil was used to repel fleas and ticks. The oil was so concentrated and effective that it worked for a month. So, after each bath, Leo got a fresh oil treatment that was applied to his head and shoulders.

Much like Leo's oil, David talked about oil being applied to the heads of the sheep in Psalm 23. It worked to rid the sheep of plaguing, tormenting insects that would burrow into their ears and drive the sheep mad. In the Bible, oil is one of the symbols of the Holy Spirit. When the Holy Spirit's thoughts are my thoughts, He brings peace from tormenting fears. Just like Leo is set free from the torment of fleas, my mind is put at ease. Oil is good stuff!

Just Sitting

Usually, when I sat down, I had an agenda of things to write, read, or sort. I have always been a firm believer in making the most of time. Leo came on the scene, and I developed a new habit. Instead of always having a task at hand, I found myself just sitting and petting Leo. It was soothing and relaxing. During these times of enjoying his company, I have experienced a new awareness of the world around me, rather than just the task before me. Listening to outdoor sounds, watching birds, and just being quiet had become my new agenda.

It's not surprising that the Lord has encouraged us to "be still and know" that He is God (Psalm 46:10). When David wrote that psalm, I wonder if he was sitting on the hillside petting his sheepdog. I can see it now. All the sheep are lazily grazing in the green pasture. David sits to rest and his dog is right there beside him. Being still gave David a song. Being still gave me this story. I wonder what will come from your time of being still.

Similarities

Many times, it has been said that dogs resemble their owners. It brought to mind imagery of a large man walking an English bulldog or a petite lady taking her recently groomed miniature poodle for a stroll. Come to think of it, though, Leo and I did have definite similarities. We both thoroughly enjoyed people of all ages, races, and sizes. Both of us were "touchy-feely" types. I was a hugger, and Leo couldn't seem to get enough petting. Having soft brown eyes was another commonality that you would notice. And oddly enough, we were both motivated by rewards of any type.

From the world of dogs, I began to see a parallel in the spirit world. We are becoming like our spiritual walking Companion. He bought and paid for us by His blood sacrifice. He has promised us that, as we walked with Him, we would become more like Him (2 Corinthians 3:18, Romans 8:29). How intriguing is that! While my common traits with Leo were just a coincidence, my becoming like Jesus was a promise.

The Door

After Leo joined my household, a top priority was to put a doggie door in the side door going into the garage. This required moving the gate of my fence forward and adding a walkway so that the entrance would be private. After a weekend of hard labor, the door was installed successfully. What a task. Now when the weather changed, which is common in Oklahoma, Leo could go inside and be safe and protected. I could be at work and not worry about the possibility of a dog being soaked in the rain or shivering in the storm.

Jesus is our spiritual Door. In John 10, we are promised that we can go in that Door and be kept safe. The Father paid quite a Price, much more than a weekend's worth of time and energy. The Father sent His absolute best and put Him in place so that we could have safety and protection from evil and harm. We have quite an Entrance, quite a Door. Come on in. The storm clouds are rising. Enter in and be safe forever!

A Licking

From my observation, it seemed that dogs treated hurts and pains by licking the wound with their tongues. In fact, that's one way I could tell something was bothering Leo. He licked his "owies." When I stayed home from work one day because of lower back pain, Leo was such a comfort to me. He sat at my feet and licked my hands and legs continuously. Usually, that's his way of showing affection. This time, however, I believe he was trying to soothe my pain.

I was reminded of the power of the tongue. Words spoken can bring life and healing or death and pain (Proverbs 18:24). My desire is to speak words that build up and encourage others. It was stirred up afresh by Mr. Licking Leo. I feel better already, especially after getting a licking.

Resting

On days I was able to stay home and work around the house, I discovered Leo's key to being so energetic. He slept all day long. He changed locations depending on where I might be, but he enjoyed the cool entryway tile the most. It's no wonder that when I came home from a hard day at work, he was all chipper and ready to play. His battery had been charging all day.

Being able to truly rest is a definite ability from the Lord, as far as we humans are concerned. It seems that the busier we are, the better. Even on the supposed "day of rest" we have our time all used up with various and sundry activities. Jesus has promised that He would give us rest if we would but come to Him (Matthew 11:28-30). Let's accept His invitation and His gift of rest. Got Jesus; got rest!

Prepared Place

I suppose you could accuse me of spoiling Leo, but it was hot outside! Leo had a doghouse, a fenced backyard, fresh water daily, and his own private entrance into our double car garage. During the summer, I moved both cars out of the garage before leaving for work. Then I closed the garage door, leaving a two to four-inch crack open. I made sure Leo's doggie door was open and, of course, the ceiling fan must be left on. Leo preferred the cool cement garage floor to the sunbaked patio. Understandable?

You might say that the Father God has spoiled His children in a similar way. Did Jesus not say, "In My Father's house are many mansions…I go to prepare a place for you" (John 14:2)? If heaven's streets are paved with gold, can you fathom what God's mansions resemble? What a prepared place. What a comforting promise. What a wonderful Father!

Skunk Expert

For about a week, I noticed that Leo was acting rather peculiar whenever he was in the garage. At first, he would sniff in just one area for quite a while. Then, he sniffed all along the edges of the garage intently as if on the trail of something. Finally, one morning I woke up to the definite odor of a skunk that seemed to be everywhere in the house, garage, and even in our cars. Leo had known about our uninvited guest for a whole week.

Just like I needed Leo's sensitive nose to warn me of an intruder in my house, I need the Holy Spirit to warn and teach me about the devil's hidden, stinky intrusions into my life. The Holy Spirit dwells inside of a believer (I John 4:13) and He knows the realm of the spirit world, both good and evil. Paying attention to His urgings will help us be aware of sneaky stinkers trying to enter into the "houses" of our lives. Praise God for giving us a spiritual skunk expert to abide in us!

Collar Time

Leo wore three different collars, for three different purposes. His tick collar stayed on constantly and was especially tight so that tick-repelling chemicals were released onto his skin. His blue collar had an identification tag on it, which included his name, address, and immunization information. Then, his third collar, a choke chain, attached to his walking leash. I put his blue collar on when I left in the mornings before he went outside or into the garage. He got excited even when I picked it up. The Leo wiggle was a common occurrence as well as soft barks of delight. Leo couldn't wait to go outside into his domain for the day.

Am I excited about the spiritual yoke or collar (Matthew 11:28-30) I have been given that connects me to Jesus? Do I delight in the fact that He and I enter my domain for the day together? I need to be, because His "yoke is easy" and His "burden is light." Why, I should be doing the Leo wiggle of joy!

A Touch

Leo was a good responder. He responded to the slightest inflection of my voice, especially to endearing words. He responded to my movements by getting up and following me around. He even responded when I simply looked his way. My attention invited him to come to me. Of all modes of expression, though, my touch said and meant the most. He appeared to devour each touch and digest it deep within his little, wiggly being.

I know the Lord is a Spirit, but I still long for His touch, His closeness. Experiencing His creation many times sets the stage for a sense of intimacy. Fellowshipping with His family brings closeness to the Father. Listening to what He has to say through His Word and prayer causes nearness as well. God's presence settles my heart. I understand Leo's insatiable longing for my hand, my words, me. I understand, for I, in like manner, can't get enough of the Presence and touch of my Lord. Join me in getting cozy with the Lord and coming away satisfied.

Clean Teeth

Growing up, dental hygiene was a top priority since I had braces, but it never crossed my mind to brush my dog's teeth. In those days, it was normal to feed and water a dog, let him gnaw on a bone occasionally, and give him a bath regularly. Leo was a different story altogether. His primary physical exam revealed a serious buildup of plaque and tartar on his back teeth. The process of laser cleaning required putting Leo to sleep. What an eye opener! My dog had special dental needs. After a year of owning Leo, brushing his teeth became a regular part of our weekly routine.

Leo's need caused me to think about my own need. I know regular maintenance is vital to keep my heart clean and tender before the Lord. Like the plaque buildup on Leo's teeth, a hardened heart is dangerous. How precious is the working, cleansing, softening power of the Blood of Jesus in our spiritual hearts. As we confess our sins (1 John 1:9), or encrusted ways, He goes in and cleans our hearts, preventing further damage. Unlike Leo's procedure, though, heart cleansing doesn't require anesthesia. Aren't you glad?

Shaven

Visits to the veterinarian were always a learning experience. This time, we learned how to identify allergic skin pustules. To see what he had felt, however, the vet had to shave Leo's belly. Fortunately, it was summer, so Leo welcomed the "cool" chest. Believe me, we could see every little bump. The plan was to rid Leo of all the obnoxious, itchy places. Two medications were prescribed and, in two weeks' time, the bumps were gone and fuzzy white hair was reappearing.

Leo's exposed skin brought to mind what Hebrews 4:13 says about how we are "open and laid bare before the eyes of Him." The Lord looks even deeper than our skin layer. As 1 Samuel 16:9 says, "The Lord looks at the heart." He knows all about us and loves us anyway. What a comfort to know that no level of exposure goes deeper than the capacity of His accepting love. He knows all and loves all.

Wellness Plan

I was well-acquainted with how insurance providers worked with doctors to cover a participating patient's needs. Upon owning a dog, however, I was ignorant of a similar "wellness plan" available for dogs. For a reasonable monthly fee, many of the routine doggie needs were covered at a lower rate. A one-time membership fee was also part of the package deal. With Leo's dental problems, I got the level of care that included dental needs as well. Such a simple, convenient plan of maintenance was helpful to an ignorant dog owner like me.

The term "wellness plan" caught my attention. The Lord has given us a similar statement of His plans in Jeremiah 29:11: "For I know the thoughts and plans that I have for you…for welfare and peace and not for evil" (AMPC). What a deal! What rich benefits supplied by a thorough and caring Father. I like His wellness plan, don't you?

Looking in the Mirror

Leo was a quick learner. He knew that when I was doing certain things, I would not respond to his cold nose nudges. For instance, my morning routine required my full attention. As I leaned over the sink in front of the mirror to put on my makeup, he had learned not to interrupt me. In fact, anytime I was facing a mirror, Leo respected my space and let me primp. Wise dog.

Even as I sit down and look into the mirror of God's Word, Leo leaves me alone. Most of the time you'll find him resting at my feet or in his bed. All of us need the time and space to gaze deeply into the Word of God. There is so much to learn and so many changes yet to be made, as we spend time listening to His voice through the written Word. Go ahead, take a good look in the mirror. Whose reflection do you see—too much of you or more of Him?

Playtime

At last, I had myself a spontaneous playmate—anytime, anywhere, and anyway! It seems to me that dogs were made to eat, sleep, go for walks, and play. Oh, the life of a dog! It never failed that at just the most inconvenient, busy time in my scheduled day, Leo wanted to play. Invariably, I condescended to his frivolity and ended up being pleasantly set free from tension and stress. It's almost like a divine setup to get my attention off business and onto fun.

Jesus knew how intense we humans tend to get, and I believe dogs are one gift He's created to help us lighten up. When He said, "Come to Me…and I will give you rest" in Matthew 11:28, one of the meanings of rest is recreation. He knew we needed a healthy mixture of work and play. I am ever learning about this proper mixture, thanks to Leo and the Lord.

Happy Trails

Although Leo was taken for walks on a regular basis and had plenty of room to run in our yard, His tail was still probably the best-developed muscle in his little body. Happy would describe his disposition during waking hours. He was happy to go outside, happy to go walking, happy to be petted, and happy to see me. In tight places, you'd think he was playing a bass drum, his tail moved so rhythmically. His tail told his heart feelings. He was as happy about being mine as I was about owning him.

In Psalm 144:15, David states, "Happy are the people whose God is the Lord!" Can others tell that I'm happy belonging to God? A cheerful, hopeful attitude is evidence of being happy. Confidence that God cares about me is another expression of happiness. One of the simplest signs, however, is the smile on my face. That's probably as close to tail wagging that we humans can get. We belong to the Lover of our souls, the Good Shepherd. Let's get to wagging about it. Others need to know, so we better show that our God makes us happy!

Moving On

Not having studied the memory capacity of a dog, I don't know what Leo remembered about his previous home and owner. We passed by that house almost daily as we took our walks. I wonder if the smells around that familiar corner spurred memories. I wonder if he recalled the lonely days, the lonely nights. Did he remember me when I would talk to him and pet him? Did he remember my hand extended under the garage door just to touch his nose? Did he remember? I couldn't tell by his actions when we went around the corner. It was as if it was just another house to him, nothing special.

Many times, I envy Leo's capacity to separate himself from what has been or used to be. As the Lord encouraged me to press on to what lies ahead, I kept looking back and longing for the security of what was familiar. It was a test of faith. God knows what lies ahead is better. That is true only as I trust in the goodness of God, even as Leo trusts in my goodness. Well, Leo's getting antsy and so am I. It's time to move farther on down the street. Let's boogie to what's better!

The Ride

I took Leo with me in the car and, once again, I learned something. A dog trainer friend of mine warned me of how the dog teaches its owner as well as vice versa. I took dog treats along to help pacify Leo during the trip. It worked, but then he wanted me to pet him. Something about my hand calmed him down and caused him to relax. Then, he would scratch the back of the seat until I reached back to give another touch. When eye contact is not possible, the hand works. Leo would lie down or even stand and gaze out the window when the road was smooth. Otherwise, he began pacing back and forth restlessly. When commanded to lie down, he would obey for a brief time before resuming his busy pace.

The Lord revealed to me that Leo was acting out what I was feeling internally. I was calm and relaxed when the road was smooth, but anxious and jittery when there were bumps, turns, and sudden stops. There's nothing like a living illustration to get the point across. It's like the Lord was saying, "Chill out! Let Me do the driving." It's a deal!

Sunning

During days off this week, I tried to remember to give Leo some "dog" time to himself. I put his collar on him, gave him a treat and let him roam his territory outside just free to be. Looking out the kitchen window or the back screen door, I found him lying down purposely in the sun's rays. One spot he chose was beside the trunk of our small redbud and another favored place was by the fence near our shed. He would change positions from facing the sun with squinted eyes to being rolled up in a foxy ball of fur. He looked so relaxed and cozy, I bundled up, moved a lawn chair and footstool out near him, and soaked up the warm rays of light with him.

I have read that when an eagle is sick or in the process of molting, he finds a high, secluded cliff and spreads himself out on a rock facing the sun. It is a private time to receive healing or strength for change. Oddly enough, aren't we faced with those same needs? Isn't the Lord our source of healing and our safe refuge during change? Malachi 4:2 says the "Sun of Righteousness (shall) arise with healing in His wings and His beams" (AMPC). Have a need? Seek the Sun and make like an eagle (or a dog).

29

Chewer

In a way, I was thankful Leo was five years old when I received him and the puppy stage was over. From previous experience, I knew how destructive tiny teeth could be on furniture, wool caps, and Bible covers. I'm convinced, however, that at age seven, Leo entered his second puppyhood. His enjoyment of rawhide toys revealed this to me. There were times he was so relaxed and content that a piece of rawhide was chewed on for hours and finally swallowed. What was disgustingly slimy to me became a delightful delicacy to him.

Interestingly enough, I find myself hungry each morning for a piece of God's Word to occupy my mind for the day. Meditation is the proper term, but it's much like Leo's chewing routine. Unlike the rawhide toy, however, God's Word gives life and I am confident of its healthy affect. I need a good chew for the day and the Lord is faithful to provide. Excuse me as I indulge.

Mark of the Beast

Amid the joys of owning and caring for Leo, there were a few minor drawbacks. One was the struggle of having a totally clean house. Regardless of how many times I vacuumed and dusted, dog hair was ever looming and lurking to land and cover once again. In spite of the diligence in washing and brushing my favored beast, he left his hairy mark everywhere. My clothes were clean... under the little hair balls here and there. Leo was so generous to share his coat all year round. Hug me; hug my dog. Visit my home; visit the home of my dog. We were inseparable in a fuzzy kind of way.

There is someone else Who not only lives with, but in us. Do we wear the evidence? The Scripture urges us to "put on the Lord Jesus Christ" (Romans 13:14). Is there evidence on or within, or have we painstakingly brushed it off or hidden it? You might want to join me in front of the mirror and check it out.

Pretty Doggie

Beauty seemed to have an underlying power. I must admit Leo was a beautifully marked Sheltie. I was not an expert. All I knew was that God did an outstanding job in color scheming Leo's fur coat. There was just the right amount of black and tan to accent the white and just the right amount of accenting in just the right places. Was that a clear enough picture? Let me put it this way: when we went for a walk, I could look as "frumpy" as I wanted, because all eyes were on the dog. Children literally came running towards Leo saying "Pretty doggie!" and wanted to pet him. I'm relieved that he had a friendly and tolerant attitude. He'd let anyone near for a touch.

I remember as a child how I was drawn to the Lord because of His beauty. The beauty of His creation was my drawing card. Beautiful songs and hymns drew me. Beautiful Christian friends drew me. Join me in responding to the Lord's beauty. As Song of Solomon 1:4 says, "Draw me away! We will run after you."

Receiver

It was not too often my own dog put me to shame, but that morning he did. As I prepared my lunch to take to work, Leo had been taught to lie down and stay on the carpet right near the kitchen. Otherwise, he would get underfoot as I went back and forth. After he endured my kitchen busyness, he knew he would be rewarded for his obedience. He waited patiently. When I came from the kitchen, I had better have the reward with me because he would look at me expectantly and get up ready to receive. At last, the cherished Cheerios were his to enjoy.

How did Leo correct me? My attitude, my expectation wasn't like his. Here I serve the God of the universe Who says, "My reward is with Me" (Revelation 22:12), and I have not been expectant.

"Lord, help me to look to You expectantly, because You are the Giver of Life. I arise to receive from You right now. I'll not have a dog outdo me!"

Following

All Leo wanted in the morning was to lie down and rest while I scurried about from room to room getting ready for work. He wasn't content to be in a room or in a spot where he couldn't open one eye and see me. Some mornings, he gave up following me around and just plopped himself down in the entryway of the office, removed from my beaten path.

How often I do the same. When the Lord is moving about and active, I simply want to take a nap or close my eyes in a quiet, out-of-the-way, secluded spot. The problem with pursuing seclusion is that God is alive, living, and active. When He moves, we are to be moving right with Him. That is what following entails: following. There are times when He leads us to lie down and rest, but being alert and ready to move with Him is vital. Let's be more alert, for we belong to a God Who is on the move.

Storms

I am not sure where Leo spent his stormy nights for the first five years of his life. Wherever it was, he was alone and uncomforted. When I first owned him, he would go bizarre during storms. He was frantic, unsettled, panting, and out-of-sorts. He would awaken or keep me awake whenever storms were brewing. Eventually, I would have to banish him to the garage so I could get some sleep. Over a period of time, I noticed a change. One night, a storm snuck up on us and Leo was determined to stay right with me. Yes, he was panting and a little restless, but he wasn't frantic.

Companionship during stormy times is so precious. The Lord has promised to be with us in trouble (Psalm 91:15). In Hebrews 13:5, He has promised to never leave us or forsake us. It takes practice and determination to remain at peace in the midst of storms, but I am learning. So is Leo. In fact, he just fell asleep at my feet and the thunderstorm is still raging.

Senior

All I knew was I needed to buy some dog food for Leo. I asked a young employee where a certain brand was located, and he asked me how old my dog was. Rather an odd question, I thought, but I told him that Leo was seven. Then, I heard the news. Leo was to now eat from the "senior" category of dog food. As he placed the large bag of food into my cart, I assured him that Leo was as frisky and playful as a puppy. He shared with me that the needs of an older dog are different and senior dog food catered to those differences. As I thought about it on the way home, I realized Leo and I were the same age, 49. Every dog year is equal to seven human years.

Yes, we are getting older, and our needs do change. How thankful I am that age doesn't faze our God. In Isaiah 46:4, He assures us: "Even to your old age, I am He, and even to gray hairs I will carry you! I have made, and I will bear; Even I will carry, and will deliver you." That promise made me want to do a cartwheel, but I can't—not in the dog food section.

Perky Ears

It was a normal spring day, and Leo and I were simply enjoying the sounds of morning. I was reading, and he had taken one of his usual sleeping spots in the grass next to the patio. Sometimes, I just got a kick out of watching him sleep, like a mother watching her child sleep and knowing all was well. Leo's eyes were closed, and his body relaxed, yet his ears were standing at attention, ready for the slightest change in the "surround sound." What a strange sleeping habit!

I sensed the Lord urging me to pay attention today to the slightest alterations in plans and directions. The prophet Isaiah put it this way: "He wakens me morning by morning, He wakens my ear to hear as a disciple [as one who is taught]" (Isaiah 50:4 AMPC). It only makes sense to me that to follow the Lord's leading, we need to remain attentive. Here I go again, receiving another object lesson from a dog. Oh, well, at least the challenge is more of a heart challenge and people won't notice my ears standing at attention. Only the Lord sees, and only Him do I seek to please.

Just a Glance

Leo was extremely sensitive, even when he was supposedly curled up to rest. Because of that, I had to be careful not to disturb him or give him signals by just looking at him. Somehow, he always had one alert eye on me and was ready to respond, ready to come, or ready to go. I suppose that much of his sensitivity was because Shelties are a type of herding breed originally bred for the purpose of herding and taking care of cattle.

What a challenge it is to follow his example as I keep my eye always on the Lord, ready to respond, ready to come, and ready to go! How I long to respond more quickly to His slightest gestures. How exciting it would be—to be led by the Lord's eyes rather than even His words. I want to be that close, sensitive, and obedient. Leo's desire has stirred afresh my own heart's desire.

"Thanks again, Lord, for instructing me through this pet You've given to me."

The Dewed

Awe! What a delight to go out on the patio in the morning after it rained the night before. The dew was especially thick on our freshly mowed lawn. Leo was making his usual rounds along the fence while I settled down to listen, read, and pray. What a refreshing way to start a day. As usual, I felt a cold nose nudging my hand and, as usual, I responded. This time, as I pet him, though, I noticed he was wet. The dew had gotten on his coat as he meandered through the tall plants in the garden. I knew where he had been.

I started wondering if I carried any evidence of where I'd been that morning. Was the refreshing dew of His presence, referred to in Hosea 6:3, evidenced in my life during that day? My desire is that others would recognize where I'd been and with Whom, and that they would desire their own "dew." How about you? "Got dew?"

Toys

Leo had some nifty toys! He had a knotted rope that he enjoyed playing tug-of-war with and then flossed his own teeth on the dangling strands. An old tennis ball intrigued him, at times, because it moved after he threw it. Then there were the basic chew bones made of hide that he gnawed on and played with for hours before eating them. When it got down to it, however, Leo would much rather have my hand touching, playing with, and rubbing him. No toy could substitute for me.

Sometimes, I wonder how long it takes me to seek God, rather than His "toys." Things are fun, and things are needed, but the Lord is my heart desire, the One I long for. May I be more persistent than Leo as I press through and leave the toys behind to get to Him. May I press in until I sense His hand and His presence with me. He alone satisfies, not all that He gives. He alone brings us joy. Let's forget the toys!

Sleepless

It was one of those nights my body just wouldn't go to sleep, regardless of how I lay or what I thought about. Finally, I got up and fixed some toast and hot tea. As usual, Leo was right behind me, watching me sleepily as I clambered around in the kitchen. One thirty isn't such a bad snack time after all. Leo ate some of his leftover food while I ate my toast and drank my tea. What a friend, to even snack with me after being awakened from a sound sleep.

There is an even better Friend who never sleeps, but watches us and is with us all the time (Psalm 121: 4). How comforting to be reminded by my furry friend about my eternal Friend. I spent time with Him this morning, early, celebrating our friendship and His constant care. Nice to know someone else was awake, too, on those sleepless nights.

Night, night, Leo.
Goodnight, Lord.

The Brushing

I don't understand how the thick hair on a Sheltie warms him in the winter and cools him in the summer. All I know is that Leo had an abundance of hair! In the summer, I brushed him painstakingly about once a week and ended up with a sizable amount of loose hair. The brushing process was vigorous, and Leo wiggled around and moaned the whole time. I was determined to loosen that thick undercoat, in spite of his resistance. Leo's playfulness afterwards let me know that he was relieved it was over.

As His sheep (Psalm 100:3), I know that the Lord has His hands full keeping our wool clean and free from worldly stuff that clings and sticks. He longs to cleanse us as often as we allow Him that privilege. He longs to free us from debris and tangles and excessive weight. Oh, how I need a good brushing and cleansing.

"I come to You, Lord. Set me free. Help me to be still and not wiggle as You work on me and in me. You are my Good Shepherd. I am Your sheep. Clean me up, Lord. Clean me up."

Fearless

My first impression of Leo was that he had a long way to go to live up to the meaning of his name, which is "bold, lion." He cowered easily and was hesitant to come when called, as if his previous owner had been abusive or rough in handling him. In no time, however, he began to change right before my eyes. He began to show confidence when he responded to my call, rather than being sheepish. When with strangers, children and other dogs, Leo's friendly nature began to blossom forth. I have even seen him show aggression towards skunks, squirrels, cats, and opossums, like quite a confident little dog. What a big change in such a short time!

The key seemed to be that Leo knew he was loved and cared for. The awareness of my love for him drove out previous fear, much like God's love drives out all fear (1 John 4:18). Resting in and being aware of the Lord's total care, provision, and unconditional love instills boldness and confidence. His love for us sets us free. His care for us sets us free. It's time we allow God's love to stir up the lion in us, for "the righteous are as bold as a lion" (Proverbs 28:1). Rise up and roar!

Walking in the Snow

Yes, I must admit that, even at my age, I still enjoyed playing in the snow. Trouble is, I hadn't found a playmate until Leo. We both enjoyed romping, playing, and even eating snow. Just tonight, we went for our evening walk into a snow-covered world. It was bright outside as we came out the front door. After a block or two, I took Leo's leash off and let him roam freely in an open field. His tri-colored fur stood out against the scenic white background.

Leo's companionship that day reminded me of a much greater Companion, the Holy Spirit (2 Corinthians 13:14). Sharing episodes of life with such a wise and comforting Person is a real privilege. In Him, we have a sure Friend with us until the end, and even beyond into eternity. Walks with Leo will end, but walks with the fellowship of the Lord will go on forever. What a Friend!

Eating Habits

I learned not to leave Leo's food outside because the ants would carry it off before he ate it. We humans have a regular eating schedule. It was odd to me how Leo ate when he was hungry, which could be anytime, day or night. His food dish had to be full and ready for consumption. I kept it in the house and made it available to him intermittently. I was fully aware of other critters that were also hungry…like mice!

How many of us could learn from Leo to eat when we are hungry? His method had been effective to keep him lean and healthy. In much the same way, we should have the food of God's Word ready and available so that we can dive in and indulge when we are hungry. Let's keep God's food from being wasted, then taste and see that the Lord is good (1 Peter 2:3), over and over again throughout the day and night. The time to eat may be right now!

Country Break

It was a last minute, spontaneous idea. Let's see, we need a leash, water, and treats. It wasn't a typical trip to the drive-in bank with Leo in the back seat. I had plans! Behind the bank was a large open field that had a gentle country feel, in the very midst of new businesses springing up all around. We would take a little country break before the heat index climbed to be unbearable. Leo was excited about the ride, despite being groggy from an interrupted routine morning nap.

Am I as eager and willing when the Lord breaks into my routine to give me a change of scenery? Am I as content to just get away and be with Him as Leo was with me? Once again, I'm learning. I'm learning. Thank you, instructor Leo. I get the picture.

"Lord, grant me the grace to simply trust Your plans and enjoy the change in scenery."

On Guard

If I said "guard dog," I'm sure you would have an image in your head of a ferocious, alert, large, intimidating German Shepherd or a similar type breed. Some people own dogs just for protection. Leo didn't know he was a miniature Collie but believed he was my protector. He saw himself as a big dog with a big responsibility to guard and manage all the area of land he could see. One morning, I spent prayer time in the front yard. First, Leo cleared out a dangerous intruder, a gray cat that ran for its life at Leo's pursuit. After that was settled, Leo lay down on the driveway in his kingly pose and looked over the territory as I continued my prayer time. Even when resting his head, his eyes remained open and searching.

Am I being as diligent as Leo to guard my God-given territory? Am I aggressively confronting the enemies of my soul before resting in peace, or am I unrealistically expecting peace with intruders present? When the Bible says to "keep your heart with all diligence" (Proverbs 4:23), Leo's behavior comes to mind. Do you want to join me on the driveway pavement? Arise, heart of a guard dog. Arise!

Lost and Found

Usually, taking Leo with me to visit my parents was a treat, but this last time it was a disaster! My parents lived in a retirement village where pets were allowed everywhere except in the dining hall. One Sunday afternoon, while dining with my parents, I left Leo at a friend's duplex. Just fifteen minutes before I came to pick him up, my friend opened the front door to greet a visitor and Leo frantically darted out the door. He was probably looking for me and afraid I had abandoned him. By the time I arrived, several people were already searching the area for him. Animal control had been called and neighbors willingly joined in the search. Cell phone numbers were exchanged, and a grueling seven hours had begun. Finally, about fifteen minutes before sunset, Leo was sighted and caught. He was tired and had lain down to rest in someone's front yard. Needless to say, he was an easy catch. Although we were all hot and exhausted, the joy of finding him was invigorating!

That day I felt, in a minuscule way, the desperate longing that the Heavenly Father must feel for His "lost" ones to be "found." Not only do I more deeply understand the parables Jesus shared about the lost sheep, the lost coin, and the lost son, I feel them. Amazing what a seven-hour lesson with Leo will do!

To the Lake or Bust

I really wanted to take Leo to the Ozarks over Labor Day weekend, but the cabin area had rules. At nine and a half years of age, could Leo prove the adage, "You can't teach an old dog new tricks," a lie? I checked with a dog expert, and he assured me Leo could still learn. First, however, my friend had to train me. I learned to proceed in front of Leo in and out of doors, and I found that a portable kennel was my new friend. After only one day of training Leo, he paused at the door to see whether I remembered to walk in before him. Amazing!

If my dog, who is about 70 years old in human years, can continue to learn new things, so can we. In Christ, we are promised that we can do all things (Philippians 4:13). Whether it's learning about a new computer, a new profession, or a new relationship, all things are possible with God (Mark 10:27). He is committed to our success, so let's get with the program. We can't let a dog show us up. Oh, yes, Leo and I will see you at the lake!

Attacked!

Leo and I were headed out for our regular morning walk when suddenly the neighbor's dog attacked him. For some unknown reason, their dog aggressively responded to Leo every time they were together. This time, however, the injuries were serious, including two wounds that needed stitching. Our leisure walk changed in a hurry. Leo visited the vet the rest of the day for a complete check-up. He was X-rayed, wounds were cleansed and stitched, antibiotics given, and pain medication administered. When I picked him up at the end of the day, he was a drowsy little fellow. Taking medicine and keeping wounds clean were added to our daily routine. He completely recovered within a month and only had a small scar under his right eye as a reminder of that day.

That incident reminded me that an attack is merely an occurrence, while healing is a process that takes time. Caring for Leo is similar to how God cares for us. He indeed "heals the broken hearted and binds up their wounds" (Psalm 147:3). Have you ever found yourself recovering from an attack? I recommend you give yourself to the One who cares for you until full recovery and beyond. He is even more dedicated to you than I am to Leo… and that's a lot!

Pain in the Paw

We were taking an early walk on a bright and cheerful Sunday morning when I noticed Leo was limping. I had seen the pieces of glass along the sidewalk area and had carefully led Leo into the grass. I thought our path was clear, but I was wrong. When I knelt to check Leo's paw, I didn't see or feel anything unusual, but I massaged and brushed off his paw and we continued our walk. His normal gait let me know that the invisible enemy was gone.

It was a quick lesson for me. As I walked through life, pain in my "paw" was a hindrance to my normal gait. Hidden hurts, known only by my Creator, had caused me to struggle to keep up my pace. Just like I noticed Leo's dilemma, I'm sure others had observed that things weren't right with me. After asking the Lord to help me, He revealed the source of my pain and set me free from it. Just as He promised in Isaiah 53:4, He took away the pain, enabling me to walk freely once again. He is such a caring Companion, so don't hesitate to get a "paw" check-up occasionally. It will save you time in the long run, or walk, whichever the case may be.

Comforter

Eight hours was a long trip. Being exhausted when I arrived home, I unpacked the car and lay down to take a nap. I had just awakened when a friend dropped in to visit. She wanted me to go with her to a party that night, but my energy level was below zero. Disappointed, she went on without me. I was feeling bad about it and went out and sat on the patio to relax, when Leo came from his cool spot by the house and just sat by me. Leo was such a comfort, such a friend. It was okay with him that my "get up and go juice had got up and went."

Leo's presence caused me to think about how the indwelling Holy Spirit is indeed our Comforter. He accepts us in weariness and in weakness and remains with us always. It's okay to need to rest. I guess that's why rest is the beginning of restore. Little Leo, with a little reminder, was a big help to me!

www.ingramcontent.com/pod-product-compliance
Lightning Source LLC
LaVergne TN
LVHW010016070426
835511LV00001B/9